W9-AZD-131

CONTENTS

FOREWORD
by Adam Hamilton

In your local community, it's likely that at least 50 percent of the people are not active in a church family. Often they consider themselves "spiritual but not religious." These are our children and grandchildren, nieces and nephews. How does God look at these non-religious people? What does God expect churches to do in order to reach out to them?

A passage of Scripture that seems pivotal in Jesus' ministry and must therefore inform our work as churches is Ezekiel 34. Through the prophet Exekiel, God speaks to the civic and religious leaders of the Jewish people and says,

> Woe to the shepherds of Israel who only take care of themselves! Should not shepherds take care of the flock? You eat the curds, clothe yourselves with the wool and slaughter the choice animals, but you do not take care of the flock. You have not strengthened the weak or healed the sik or bound up the injured. You have not brought back the strays or searched for the lost. You have ruled them harshly and brutally. So they were scattered because there was no shepherd, and

when they were scattered they became food for all the wild animals. My sheep wandered over all the mountains and on every high hill. They were scattered over the whole earth, and no one searched or looked for them. I myself will search for my sheep and look after them. As a shepherd looks after his scattered flock when he is with them, so will I look after my sheep. I will rescue them from all the places where they were scattered on a day of clouds and darkness. I will bring them out from the nations and gather them from the countries, and I will bring them into their own land. I will pasture them on the mountains of Israel, in the ravines and in all the settlements in the land. I will tend them in a good pasture, and the mountain heights of Israel will be their grazing land. There they will lie down in good grazing land, and there they will feed in a rich pasture on the mountains of Israel. I myself will tend my sheep and have them lie down, declares the Sovereign Lord. I will search for the lost and bring back the strays. I will bind up the injured and strengthen the weak, but the sleek and the strong I will destroy. I will shepherd the flock with justice. (Ezekiel 34: 2-5, 11-16).

I believe it was this passage that Jesus had in mind when he said "I am the good shepherd" (John 10:11). Matthew noted that when Jesus looked at the multitudes he had compasion on them because they were "like sheep without a shepherd" (Matthew 9:36). Jesus devoted most of his time to seeking to minister to people who were lost sheep. I believe he was revealing his own heart when he spoke of the shepherd who had one hundred sheep, but who left the ninety-nine behind to "go after the [one] lost sheep until he [found] it" (Luke 15:4). The text goes on to say that when he has found the sheep "he joyfully puts it on his shoulders and goes home. Then he calls his friends and neighbors together and says, 'Rejoice with me; I have found my lost sheep.' I tell you that in the same way there will be more rejoicing in heaven over one sinner who repents than over ninety-nine righteous persons who do not need to repent" (Luke 15:5-7). Notice the prevalence of joy that comes in finding lost sheep!

Another metaphor Jesus used is that of a fisher. He saw himself as a man fishing for people. His fishing was "catch and release." Imagine Jesus catching fish from a small pond filled with scum and silt and algae and then releasing them in to the deep and fresh waters of the Kingdom of God. Jesus' call to his first disciples and still to us today is, "Come, follow me . . . and I will send you out to fish for people" (Mark 1:16-18).

As I've been writing this, I've been sitting by a pond where a friend of mine brought his four-and-a-half year old grandson to fish. They've carefully chosen the right spot to fish (into the wind) and have brought a variety of lures to try. They cast their lines into the water and slowly reel them in. Most of the time they catch nothing, but today the fish are biting. And every ten minutes or so either the boy or his grandfather shouts, "I've got one, I've got one!" Talk about joy! It doesn't get any better than this for a grandfather and his grandson.

The mission of our churches is to continue the mission of Jesus. We are meant to continue the search for the lost sheep. We are meant to continue to fish for people. And there is incredible joy in finding lost sheep and in fishing for people.

I got in my car one Sunday after church and found that someone had left a note on my seat that read, "Pastor Adam, thank you for leading a church that would change the course of my life over the years. How I dated, how I treat my wife, how I now raise my son—these are all different because I became a Christian here in this church. I am eternally grateful."

I felt joy in reading his note, but the note itself expressed the joy this man had found in meeting and following the Good Shepherd and from swimming in God's seas.

This book was written to encourage you as you seek to lead your church to "bring back the strays and search for the lost." It is a guide to fishing for people. But finding the strays and fishing for people is not merely about technique; it is about cultivating a love for lost sheep and discovering the joy of fishing for people. After an hour of fishing, Drake and his grandpa are heading home. They caught twelve fish altogether. Their hands were a bit smelly and their bodies were a bit sweaty—this happens when you're fishing. But as the boy walked to the car he turned to me and said, "That was AWESOME!"

As your congregation rediscovers the joy of fishing, and they begin to see people's lives changed through the ministry of your church, I suspect you'll hear them say, "That was AWESOME!"

WELCOME TO *CATCH*

This book was written to encourage you to be a church that fishes for people. As you will read, those who have said yes to a life with Jesus have a great responsibility for living out that commitment. Over the course of the Catch program, you and your leaders will be working to transform your entire church—the building, the members, even the parking lot—into a visitor-friendly, outward-focused, hospitable community. You may discover gifts, talents, and passions that could help your church carry out Jesus' call to fish for people. As you dive into the daily readings that follow, listen for the whisper of the Holy Spirit. Pay attention to what God might be calling you to do.

But remember, fishing for people is not about technique; it is about cultivating a love for lost sheep and discovering the joy of drawing people to a life with Jesus Christ. The mission of our churches is to continue the mission of Jesus. We are meant to fish for people. You'll find, if you haven't already, that there is incredible delight in doing so. As your congregation discovers the joy of fishing, may you see lives changed through the relentlessly outward focus of your church.

A GUIDE TO THE DAILY READINGS

Daily readings are designed to be followed from Monday (Day One) through Saturday (Day Six), with a group meeting on the seventh day. You are welcome to structure your schedule in a way that works best for you. The important thing is to make a commitment to read daily and to bring your best thoughts and efforts to each group meeting.

As you prepare for your commitment to the daily readings, you may find the following steps helpful.

1. Commit to a scheduled time to read and reflect each day. Set aside about 15-20 minutes.

2. Find a quiet place free from interruptions.

3. Begin in prayer, asking God to speak to you through the daily readings. You might pray a simple prayer such as this:

Dear God, I want to know, love, and serve you more. As I study your word today, open my mind to discover what it means to fish for people as you have called me to do. Help me to build up the church by using my gifts. Amen.

4. Read the Scripture passage. You may want to read the verses before and after the selected passage for additional context and meaning. You can also read the Scripture in different translations, using an online resource such as www.biblegateway.com.

5. As you go through the day's reading, make notes of your thoughts. Respond to the questions on paper rather than answer them mentally. You will find this enriches your experience.

6. Be prepared to share your thoughts, questions, and reflections when your group meets each week.

WEEK 1
BECOMING RELENTLESSLY OUTWARD FOCUSED

Day One

Isn't It Wonderful How Small and Cozy We Are?

The Human One came to seek and save the lost.
Luke 19:10

When my church was founded, the pastor stood before the congregation to tell us that we were going to be focused on people outside our doors. Our church would be known for our concern for reaching those who didn't know God's love, or who may have forgotten. Our young church was passionate about our mission—but only for a brief period. Not long after we received that charge, one of our leaders spoke up in a leadership team meeting. He told the group that he liked how small and cozy we were, that he wanted to stay the size we were, at that moment. My pastor looked around the room and saw nodding heads, indicating his leadership team was in agreement. Somehow over the course of just a few weeks we had gone from being completely committed to outreach to having an inward focus on ourselves and our own needs.

Have you noticed how easy it is to lose our focus on people outside our walls and instead be focused on our own needs in church and what we hope to get out of it? We forget our mission to reach out and connect with visitors or those who don't attend a church.

Jesus never confused his purpose. His entire ministry was about seeking out and saving lost people. Luke 19:10 tells us that Jesus came to seek out and to save the lost. Matthew 9:35-36 reminds us that he did not focus only on those who had already decided to follow him; instead he demonstrated an outward approach:

> Jesus traveled among all the cities and villages, teaching in their synagogues, announcing the good news of the kingdom, and healing every disease and every sickness. Now when Jesus saw the crowds, he had compassion for them because they were troubled and helpless, like sheep without a shepherd.

As the church, we are the body of Christ. We are called to have the same heart as Christ, one filled with compassion for lost people. We exist to proclaim the good news to people who may never have heard it or who have heard it and forgotten. And though we may sometimes forget it, our mission remains.

Christ empowered the church to carry out the mission he began on earth—to seek and save the lost. This simple statement covers a broad ministry, as the lost includes all who suffer, from physical slavery to simply lacking an ultimate purpose in life. With this broad view of the mission, it is easy to see how the whole body, not just preachers and pastors, must be involved and committed to the mission in order for the church to carry out its calling.

Let's think back to the church leader's desire for a small and cozy church. Very few of us would admit that our church is like that. We think we are friendly enough. We think we want to reach out to people. We think that people should want to come and visit. But most often we aren't truly, actively seeking the lost. We hang out our OPEN sign and hope that people will show up. We say with our words that we want to grow and want non-Christian or non-churchgoing people to experience God in our churches. But our actions don't always match our words. We want to grow, but we don't want to give up our seats. We want to grow, but we are frustrated by traffic in the parking lot. We want to grow, but... (insert excuse here).

This week we are going to focus on becoming relentlessly outward focused and having a selfless commitment to Jesus' mission for the church—seeking and saving lost people. So, think about your own church. Are you excited about rallying your congregation and living out the mission to which you are called? Are you ready to become relentlessly outward focused?

- Are you open to growth, or do you secretly hope to stay small and cozy?
- What do you imagine when you think of your church becoming relentlessly outward focused?

DAY TWO

HERE IS THE CHURCH, HERE IS THE STEEPLE...

The LORD's word came to me: Human one, prophesy against Israel's shepherds. Prophesy and say to them, The LORD God proclaims to the shepherds: Doom to Israel's shepherds who tended themselves! Shouldn't shepherds tend the flock? You drink the milk, you wear the wool, and you slaughter the fat animals, but you don't tend the flock. You don't strengthen the weak, heal the sick, bind up the injured, bring back the strays, or seek out the lost; but instead you use force to rule them with injustice. Without a shepherd, my flock was scattered; and when it was scattered, it became food for all the wild animals. My flock strayed on all the mountains and on every high hill throughout all the earth. My flock was scattered, and there was no one to look for them or find them.

Ezekiel 34:1-6

Most of us know the children's rhyme: "Here is the church, and here is the steeple. Open the doors and see all the people." You probably remember closing your fists, hiding your fingers inside, then opening the doors to reveal all the people.

When you reflect on this idea, though—that you have to open the doors to see the people—you might start to question its meaning. Why is the church hidden behind such tightly closed fists? Why do you have to open the doors to see the people? Maybe the rhyme should begin with open hands and wiggling fingers, and maybe the words should say: "Here is the church; see all the people, who open the doors to welcome new people."

As the body of Christ, we have a great responsibility to represent God's physical and moral presence in the world—to be outwardly focused, going into the community, casting the net wide, reaching lost people for Christ. We should be churches with open doors, welcoming new people. But too often, the church that new people experience is the church represented in this children's rhyme by our tightly interlocked hands. New people arrive and encounter a closed door, and when they walk inside they see a church full of people who seem to be focused more on their own needs than the needs of others. We don't intentionally start out to be churches hidden in closed fists; it happens gradually, and many times we don't recognize that this is the type of church we have become.

In order to become a relentlessly outward-focused church, we have to take on the heart of God. In the Scripture above, Ezekiel gives us a picture of what the heart of God looks like. He was writing during the Jewish exile in Babylon, when the Jewish people wondered why God had let the Babylonians conquer them. Their temple had been destroyed, their capital city had been ruined, and they had been carried away as slaves. In this chapter Ezekiel tells them why: The leaders of Israel, the shepherds of God's people, failed to seek out and live in tune with the heart of God. Instead, they focused on their own needs.

Living in tune with the heart of God means that we care for the weak, sick, and injured; bring back those who have strayed; and search for those who are lost. That is the work set before us. Sometimes, though, we are like the leaders Ezekiel was writing to. We lose our focus. Our work has dwindled to simply maintaining our building and our programs.

But God's message in Ezekiel is clear: We are called to be in our communities seeking the lost, caring for the weak and the sick— sharing the very heart of God.

- How is your church doing at sharing the heart of God?
- What are some simple steps you could take to do a better job?

DAY THREE

FISHING FOR PEOPLE

As Jesus walked alongside the Galilee Sea, he saw two brothers, Simon, who is called Peter, and Andrew, throwing fishing nets into the sea, because they were fishermen. "Come, follow me," he said, "and I'll show you how to fish for people." Right away, they left their nets and followed him.

Matthew 4:18-20

People with fishing experience know that certain bait will attract a certain type of fish, but not another. Stinkbait, a breadball, or even a simple worm is a tasty treat for catfish or perch. But if you want to reel in a bass, use a live minnow or a shiny spinner lure. To increase the odds for success, cast the minnow or lure toward the shore in the shallow water where bass feed. Crappie also like minnows, but not cast in the same place as for bass. To catch crappie, cast the minnow deep in the water and keep it still until they take notice. Successful fishermen know that one single style of bait is not effective for attracting all the different fish in a particular body of water. It takes a tackle box filled with a variety of baits, lures, and weights to land a good catch.

Those who fish also know the value of research. They rely on reports provided by experts who analyze the local bodies of water and supply important information about the current fishing conditions, such as what species of fish are biting, where, and on what bait. Sure, the novice may walk out to the water with a pole and catch a fish or two, but those with a well-equipped tackle box and proper research will be more successful.

When Jesus approached Simon and Andrew, he was dealing with two men who were fishing experts. To them, fishing was not a hobby or sport. It was their livelihood. They knew the best times and places to fish. They knew the best techniques. They knew what kind of boat and equipment would afford them the biggest catch. They knew how to catch fish. Jesus invited them into his ministry and asked them to "fish for people," to take all they knew about fishing and apply it to reaching people with the love of God.

Have you ever considered that fishing for people is the livelihood of our churches as well? Sometimes we leave this job to the evangelism committee, and the rest of us make excuses: we are too shy; we are too busy; we don't know what to say; we don't like the idea of pushing our faith on other people. But if our churches—whole congregations, not just pastors and leaders—embrace this job, fishing for people who need to know the saving love of God in Jesus Christ, we'll feel alive like we never have before.

Jesus invited Simon and Andrew into an exciting new ministry, and he calls us to that very same work. As you reflect on Jesus' invitation to fish for people, consider what it might mean for you personally and for your church.

- How are you fishing for people in your daily life?
- What would your church look like if everyone took seriously Jesus' call to fish for people?

Day Four

We Are the Church Together

If I speak in tongues of human beings and of angels but I don't have love, I'm a clanging gong or a clashing cymbal. If I have the gift of prophecy and I know all the mysteries and everything else, and if I have such complete faith that I can move mountains but I don't have love, I'm nothing. If I give away everything that I have and hand over my own body to feel good about what I've done but I don't have love, I receive no benefit whatsoever.

Love is patient, love is kind, it isn't jealous, it doesn't brag, it isn't arrogant, it isn't rude, it doesn't seek its own advantage, it isn't irritable, it doesn't keep a record of complaints, it isn't happy with injustice, but it is happy with the truth. Love puts up with all things, trusts in all things, hopes for all things, endures all things.

Love never fails. As for prophecies, they will be brought to an end. As for tongues, they will stop. As for knowledge, it will be brought to an end. We know in part and we prophesy in part; but when the perfect comes, what is partial will be brought to an end. When I was a child, I used to speak like a child, reason like a child, think like a child. But now that I have become a man, I've put an end to childish things. Now we see a reflection in a mirror; then we will see face-to-face. Now I know partially, but then I will know completely in the same way that I have been completely known. Now faith, hope, and love remain—these three things—and the greatest of these is love.

1 Corinthians 13

The Scripture passage today is often read at weddings. Couples view it as the ideal of what marital love should be like. It is the standard for a love between two people that is committed and generous, that will see them through rich times and poor times, in sickness and in health. The passage works well for this purpose. It also applies beautifully to love among families, siblings, and friends.

The passage was originally written, though, not about romantic love or love between friends, but about love that people shared within a community. It was written to a church whose members were struggling to love one another. They had allowed petty bickering and power struggles to infect their community and compromise their ministry. You can imagine how they were treating one another by observing all the negative adjectives used in the letter: love is not envious, boastful, arrogant, or rude. If this is the way they were behaving, you can see why they were having problems. This first letter to the Corinthians, and especially this passage, was written to remind them how to treat one another as they lived in community.

Sometimes as church members we do not love each other so well. Maybe one member hurts another member's feelings, so we lash out. Sometimes we speak harshly to one another in meetings. Usually the problem stems from self-centered motives and pride.

There will be times when we disagree with a sermon, a resolution, even a decision to change from Pepsi to Coke machines. Some conflict is normal, but it's how we respond and live with the conflict that keeps us focused inward or relentlessly outward.

How we love and care for one another in the church family is both a reflection of a close relationship with God and an example of God's love to those outside the church. People will be drawn to a community where people treat one another with kindness, respect, and patience, in large part because these qualities are so rare in the world. At work, people face tough competition and an unrelenting drive for efficiency and productivity. Often their homes are anything but peaceful and life-giving. If the church, in contrast, is a place that is affirming, loving, and giving, a place where hope and peace are found, then people will be open to hearing and experiencing God's presence. In fact, the way we behave toward each other may be our most effective means of spreading the good news of Jesus Christ.

- How have you experienced disappointment in church relationships?
- Why does your church's love for one another matter to those who don't go to church?

Day Five

Looking for the Lost

*Jesus told them this parable: "Suppose someone among you
had one hundred sheep and lost one of them. Wouldn't he leave
the other ninety-nine in the pasture and search for the lost one
until he finds it? And when he finds it, he is thrilled and places
it on his shoulders. When he arrives home, he calls together
his friends and neighbors, saying to them, 'Celebrate with me
because I've found my lost sheep.' In the same way, I tell you,
there will be more joy in heaven over one sinner who changes
both heart and life than over ninety-nine righteous people who
have no need to change their hearts and lives."*

Luke 15:1-7

In Luke 15, Jesus tells three different stories about lost things: the
lost sheep, the lost coin, and the lost son. In the stories, the lost things
are irreplaceable treasures that, when found, bring about a celebration.
The stories not only tell us how much God treasures each of us but also
how we are called to seek out the lost in this world.

When you read Jesus' words about leaving ninety-nine sheep to
go and look for one, you might think to yourself that losing one sheep
out of a hundred is not that big a deal. You might think the shepherd
should just forget about that one and focus on the ninety-nine he has
before him. But that is not the way God operates. God doesn't write off
people who aren't in the fold; instead he pursues them, searches for
them, and throws a party when they're found. Jesus shares with us the
stories about lost things to teach us about our mission and purpose in
this world.

When we are relentlessly outward focused, we seek out every
chance to communicate—with or without words—God's love to those
who may know nothing of it. We search high and low to connect with
people who need love and grace. We might think of evangelism only as
telling people about Jesus, when in fact there are many ways to share

God's love in the world. We are called to keep our eyes open and seek out opportunities to find people who are in need of a fresh experience of God. Here are a few ideas to get you thinking:

At Work

The workplace opens opportunities for service and sharing God's love that never come our way within the confines of the church and its ministries. In the course of daily business, we will cross paths with people who may not take the church seriously. Whether we relate to them as employer or employee, customer or service provider, we may be the only people God can use to touch their lives. With this in mind, we should carry ourselves with a spirit of love and service in all our dealings.

At Home

Unlike those at work, relationships at home tend to be long-term, which magnifies their potential for blessing and serving but also for pain and hurt. It can be incredibly difficult to maintain a servant's spirit toward parents who have treated us badly; a rebellious, uncooperative child; or a spouse with a hurtful addiction that has interrupted our lives. Loving others does not mean co-dependency—God does not want us to be doormats. But in homes filled with light and love, as well as in those where challenges and pain intrude, we are called to act in love and demonstrate the grace of God.

In the Community

When one of his opponents asked Jesus to define who exactly was his neighbor, Jesus responded with the story of the Good Samaritan. Our neighbors are those who cross our path in need of love, grace, and care. When we keep our eyes open, we find that just about everyone we meet could use a kind word, a prayer, and an act of service, or simple grace.

- Are your eyes open to search for ways to minister at work, at home, and in the community?
- How can you share God's love with someone who doesn't know God this week?

Day Six

Relentless and Ready

Instead, regard Christ as holy in your hearts. Whenever anyone asks you to speak of your hope, be ready to defend it. Yet do this with respectful humility, maintaining a good conscience. Act in this way so that those who malign your good lifestyle in Christ may be ashamed when they slander you.

1 Peter 3:15-16

Who told you about Jesus? Who influenced you to decide to follow him? It may have been one person, or it may have been many people, playing different parts at different times in your life. It may have been a preacher addressing a large audience or a friend sitting with you over coffee.

However it happened for you, hearing about Jesus is something that has gone on for over two thousand years. The New Testament has a word for one person telling another about Jesus: *euangelizo,* which is a Greek word meaning "to share good news." What better news could there be to share than Jesus' love, grace, and victory over death? The Greek word may sound somewhat familiar to you, as it is the root of the English words *evangelize* and *evangelist.*

Unfortunately, the word evangelist can sometimes conjure images of a charismatic but unscrupulous Elmer Gantry character. Some even forget that the word ever existed without the prefix tele attached to it! But, biblically, evangelizing means one person sharing the good news of Jesus with someone else. This is a particularly powerful and life-changing way to relentlessly look outward and reach people with the love of God.

However we feel about the word evangelism, it is something to which all Christians are called. Ephesians 4:11 says that Christ gave some of us a special giftedness for sharing Christ with others, though in many different ways. British writer John Stott suggests that the gift of evangelism may be defined by traits such as making the gospel accessible to unbelievers or assisting those who have been hesitant to finally make a commitment to Christ. More than likely, the gift of evangelism is identified by these characteristics as well as others.

Even though Ephesians tells us that God gave "some" the spiritual gift of evangelism, that does not mean the rest of us can forget about sharing our faith. In today's reading, Peter urges all of us, not just some of us, to "always be prepared to give an answer to everyone who asks" about the hope we have in Jesus Christ. If you have the gift of approaching total strangers and effectively sharing the good news, by all means use it. But if you break into a cold sweat at the thought of doing so, be assured that you will find other opportunities to share your faith as you look relentlessly outward. Inevitably, some day someone will ask you, "How come you seem so peaceful?" or "Do you really believe that story about Jesus' resurrection?" At those moments, Peter says, be ready to give an answer. Watch for those occasions, and ask the Holy Spirit to help you when they come. Often, God uses this type of sharing to reach people who are too closed off or scared or skeptical to listen to a gifted evangelist. Sometimes a quiet word of sharing from a trusted friend or co-worker is God's best chance to break through.

- How do you feel about describing yourself as an evangelist?
- With whom do you need to share your faith?

WEEK 2
ANSWERING THREE IMPORTANT QUESTIONS

DAY ONE

WHY DO PEOPLE NEED JESUS?

*So we try to persuade people, since we know what it means to
fear the Lord. We are well known by God, and I hope that in
your heart we are well known by you as well. We aren't trying
to commend ourselves to you again. Instead, we are giving you
an opportunity to be proud of us so that you could answer
those who take pride in superficial appearance, and not in
what is in the heart.*

*If we are crazy, it's for God's sake. If we are rational, it's for
your sake. The love of Christ controls us, because we have con-
cluded this: one died for the sake of all; therefore, all died. He
died for the sake of all so that those who are alive should live
not for themselves but for the one who died for them and was
raised.*

2 Corinthians 5:11-15

After college, I worked for a nationally known department store.
One of my responsibilities was sales training for new store associates. During the training, I asked each new associate to select a product from the department where they would be working so we could
simulate an encounter with a customer. I played the role of customer,
and the sales associate's job was to convince me that the product they
were selling was something I needed.

Of course, being a normal customer, my first response as they
approached was, "I'm just looking." An ineffective salesperson would
take that response at its surface level and leave me unattended as I continued my browsing, and eventually I would decide either to leave the
store without the product or to approach the associate and ask a question about the product. Most often when I asked, "Can you tell me
about this particular feature?" the ineffective associate would respond,
"I don't have any personal experience with this particular product, but

I understand it works this way." As a customer, this normally dampened my interest in the product.

Many times after debriefing the experience with the sales associate, I would discover one of two things. (1) They knew nothing about the product they had selected. They hadn't taken the time to learn about it, read about its features, or experience it personally. (2) They simply were not passionate about what they were selling. They may have known something about the product, but they didn't really believe in it.

Compare that experience with one of an effective sales associate. The effective associate would find ways to engage me in conversation, eventually leading to a discussion about the product I was exploring. During this conversation the associate would share knowledge about the benefits of the product, along with personal stories or experiences of satisfaction, suggesting that I might also experience this same satisfaction with the product, ultimately leaving me convinced that the product was something I truly needed.

What is the difference between the effective and the ineffective salesperson? The effective salesperson took the time to learn about the product, shared their personal experiences regarding the benefits it had to offer, and was passionate about telling others.

As followers of Jesus, we are called to persuade people to come and follow him. We are his "sales force" here on earth. In the Scripture for today, Paul is demonstrating his effective selling skills. He was knowledgeable about the benefits of the new life to which he was referring. His passion was motivated by love, and he was able to share persuasively the benefits of this new life from his own personal experience. He knew his "customers" and was able to convince them that this new life was the answer to their questions and needs.

Today, people still seek an answer to the question of how to live a better life. Week after week they just keep looking. They are looking for purpose in their lives, relationships with others, relief from their anxiety and depression. They are looking for hope after a cancer diagnosis or for life after losing a loved one. Whatever they are looking for, they want and need something that will meet their hearts' deepest longings.

Do you believe passionately that people need Jesus Christ?

- What are the benefits of a life with Jesus? How is your life changed for the better because you belong to him?
- How will you find ways to tell the people you know about the amazing things God has done in your life?

Day Two

Telling People About Jesus

The man answered, "I don't know whether he's a sinner.
Here's what I do know: I was blind and now I see."

John 9:25

Reflect for a moment on the last time you shared your faith or invited someone to join you at church. Maybe you brought someone this past Sunday, maybe it was a few weeks ago, may it was a year ago, or...maybe even longer.

Why is it that we easily recommend a great restaurant, movie, book, or dress boutique but take pause before we recommend a life with Jesus or invite someone to church? Perhaps you invited someone before, and they didn't come. Maybe you want to invite someone but are afraid they might turn you down. Everyone knows you go to church; so, if they are interested they will ask. Right?

Somehow over the course of time we lose our passion for sharing what God has done for us. We become complacent. We become comfortable. We move into a maintenance mode—go to church, dabble in Bible study, serve on committees. It's not intentional, but over time, sometimes, it happens.

The story in today's Bible reading is about a total life change. The man in the story was blind before he met Jesus, and then he received sight. In fact, that's pretty much all he knows about Jesus. He doesn't know the theological implications of what happened. He can't explain the historical significance. He can't really even tell the Jewish leaders how it happened. He can only tell them that he was blind and now he can see. That is quite a story to tell.

You may not have an expertly crafted, theologically astute explanation of why you have given your life to Christ. You may not have experienced a dramatic physical healing like the blind man in the Bible story. But you do have a story to tell about why you have chosen to follow Jesus. Think about that story this week. Make some notes in your journal or Bible. Consider what your life was like before you met Jesus, what Jesus did in your life, and what your life looks like now as you walk with him.

Now think about people you know who need to hear that story. Imagine places where you might have opportunities to share. How can you be ready to communicate that story whenever an opportunity arises?

Consider another story, about a pastor who got caught reading a pocket testament on a plane. After the flight attendants had finished their duties, one walked past him and said,

"Reading a good book?"

He answered, "Yes, have you ever read it?"

She replied, "I tried once, but it was too hard to understand."

And so he said, "Well, let me tell you what I do when I read it. First, I pray, 'God just show me one thing from this chapter. Help me see and understand just one thing from this chapter.' Then, when I read the chapter, I don't worry about the things I don't understand. I just look for one verse I do understand. Then I read that verse again and I think, 'What does this verse mean to me?' "

The flight attendant said, "That's a really good idea. Maybe I'll try that."

Now, the pastor could have stopped the conversation there and gone back to reading. But instead he said, "Do you go to church anywhere?"

She said, "No, I used to go to church when I was younger, but when I got older I never could find a church that I really liked."

Very gently he told her, "You know, I understand it's hard to find a great church, but here's what I think is really important about going to church, and here's how it changed my life."

At that point, the pilot came on the intercom and asked everyone to be seated for landing. During the landing, the pastor wrote a note in the front of his pocket testament. Then he went through each book of the testament and circled his favorite verses. As they were leaving the plane, he told the flight attendant, "I want to give you my pocket testament. Would that be okay?" Surprised, she thanked him.

Evangelism is not about pounding someone over the head. It is demonstrating tangibly the love of Christ to those around you, for when they see your love, grace, and hospitality, they may just say, "Hey, I want more of that."

- What does evangelism mean to you? What would your version of evangelism look like?
- Challenge yourself to tell your faith story to someone this week, and invite him or her to church with you.

Day Three

Why Do People Need the Church?

Now when Jesus came to the area of Caesarea Philippi, he asked his disciples, "Who do people say the Human One is?"

They replied, "Some say John the Baptist, others Elijah, and still others Jeremiah or one of the other prophets."

He said, "And what about you? Who do you say that I am?"

Simon Peter said, "You are the Christ, the Son of the living God."

Then Jesus replied, "Happy are you, Simon son of Jonah, because no human has shown this to you. Rather my Father who is in heaven has shown you. I tell you that you are Peter. And I'll build my church on this rock. The gates of the underworld won't be able to stand against it."

Matthew 16:13-18

Today's Scripture reading is the first time the word church appears in the Bible. Jesus was calling the church into existence from a group of people who, to everyone including themselves, probably looked less than capable of doing so. Yet they were brought together for a purpose. Jesus called them out.

The word church comes from the Greek word *ekklesia,* which means a gathering of people who have been called out for a special purpose. Jesus was the first to apply this word to his disciples, who understood their role of continuing the calling of God's people in the Old Testament as a kingdom of priests. This definition of the Greek word fits, but it is not the complete picture. The disciples were the beginning of a new movement, one that invites people to join in a body that has a unique relationship to God through Jesus Christ.

When Jesus refers to the church he is not speaking of a building or a specific denomination, but rather to all people who follow him. He establishes his church with Peter and the other disciples. Jesus was, and continues to be, the builder; and so the church is dependent upon his power alone. Because the church was built by the power of Jesus, he could say confidently that it would withstand even the gates of Hades. In New Testament times, Hades was believed by Romans to be the realm of the dead, so Jesus was declaring that even death could not vanquish the church.

Whenever I hear stories of Christians around the world who gather for worship and study together while under the threat of violence or persecution for their beliefs, I am in awe. I wonder whether my faith would prove that strong and true, and I also marvel that the church not only survives but thrives in conditions created to squelch it.

In light of today's Bible passage, though, it should not be surprising that the church thrives, because in establishing the church Jesus promised that no power would overcome his power, that nothing would destroy his church. It is humbling to know that any success of the church is attributed to God's strength and not to ours; it is also incredibly exciting to participate in something ultimately powerful and eternal.

Today Jesus still invites us to participate in the building and continuing of the church. Our purpose as the church is to make Christ known to the world. By joining the church, you say yes to the church's mission in the world.

There is a difference between coming to church and being the church. Instead of looking at the church as a place where you can have your needs met, you begin to view it as a place where you can meet the needs of others—those who are oppressed, who hunger physically and spiritually, who are lonely and hurting—those for whom Christ died.

As you consider why people need the church, start thinking about why you need it. How do you feel called to live out your faith in the community of people who believe in Jesus and follow him?

- Why do you need the church? Why do others need it?
- Why do you think Jesus chose to create a church—an entire community—instead of just one or two key people?

DAY FOUR

PASSION OF THE CROWD

Once again David assembled the select warriors of Israel, thirty thousand strong. David and all the troops who were with him set out for Baalah, which is Kiriath-jearim of Judah, to bring God's chest up from there—the chest that is called by the name of the LORD of heavenly forces, who sits enthroned on the winged creatures. They loaded God's chest on a new cart and carried it from Abinadab's house, which was on the hill. Uzzah and Ahio, Abinadab's sons, were driving the new cart. Uzzah was beside God's chest while Ahio was walking in front of it. Meanwhile, David and the entire house of Israel celebrated in the LORD's presence with all their strength, with songs, zithers, harps, tambourines, rattles, and cymbals.

King David was told, "The LORD has blessed Obed-edom's family and everything he has because of God's chest being there." So David went and brought God's chest up from Obed-edom's house to David's City with celebration. Whenever those bearing the chest advanced six steps, David sacrificed an ox and a fatling calf. David, dressed in a linen priestly vest, danced with all his strength before the LORD. This is how David and the entire house of Israel brought up the LORD's chest with shouts and trumpet blasts.

2 Samuel 6:1-5, 12-15

The first time I attended a Kansas City Chiefs football game, I suffered culture shock. Fanatic does not even begin to describe the typical person at a Chiefs game. Hours before the kickoff, thousands of people gather in the parking lot to tailgate. Smoke billows into the sky from all the barbeque grills, and the smell of brats and hamburgers fills the air. People mingle between cars, make new friends, share food, and swap stories. A few hours later, the stadium is filled with tens of thousands of people dressed in red and white, trying to get as close to the front as possible, standing on their feet, jumping up and down, clapping their hands, and yelling as loudly as they can. People I know to be respectable members of society, including my senior pastor, act with unbridled passion and devotion. And this is before the game even starts.

Contrast that with another type of gathering held across the country each weekend. People come to worship, slowly shuffling to find seats in the back of the room. Their arms are crossed. Many ignore their neighbors. In fact, a large number do not even arrive on time; instead they enter the sanctuary ten or fifteen minutes after the service starts. They stand for the singing but barely make a sound. Some of these people may be the same ones who cheered the loudest at the previous day's football game. What happened to all their enthusiasm?

Although not the most moral or upright man, King David loved God with all his heart. He was known for his passionate, unfettered worship of God. In today's passage from Second Samuel, David was celebrating the Ark of the Covenant's return to the Israelites, reclaimed from their enemies. The ark was a physical representation of the presence of God. David was excited about bringing the ark to Jerusalem, the capital city and home to his palace, because it signified that Israel was under God's rule and protection, the Lord was the true king, and David was God's handpicked servant. He was so excited, in fact, that he acted in a completely undignified manner, as his wife later pointed out to him. He danced in the streets like a commoner, not even worried about the state of his clothes.

When we gather as the church to worship, we gather to celebrate. Our corporate identity comes from naming who God is, knowing who we are before God, and remembering all that God has done for us. We welcome God's presence among us. Like the football fans, when we arrive early to worship, with anticipation, it affects the spirit of the entire group. Like David, when we let go of our facades and inhibitions we are able to bring our whole hearts, bodies, and spirits to our worship, so that God may do great things in and through us. And though personal time with God is important, the gathered church is who God made us to be. When we worship, gather to serve, share common space and common meals, we experience with greater intensity the fire of God's spirit. In this way we learn from, inspire, and encourage one another.

Through the group, God can show us a vision that is sometimes more difficult to hear on our own.

- How do you approach church gatherings? With excitement and anticipation, or with feelings of obligation?
- How can you demonstrate to those on the outside that the church is an exciting place to be?

Day Five

Why Do People Need Your Church?

Then the church throughout Judea, Galilee, and Samaria en-
joyed a time of peace. God strengthened the church, and its
life was marked by reverence for the Lord. Encouraged by the
Holy Spirit, the church continued to grow in numbers.

Acts 9:31

Families are important. We share meals together; help one another
with projects; gather to celebrate holidays, birthdays, and anniver-
saries; vacation together; and sometimes simply sit and have conversation. Families are strengthened because of these times together. If a
member of the family is not present, others often notice and miss that
person's contribution.

Realizing that a young man had stopped attending church, one of
my pastors made contact with him. The young man reported that he
had attended for several years but then quit coming, not because anything had offended him or because he no longer believed in God but
because he felt that he had "learned everything" he needed to know
and saw no reason to keep attending. The strength of belonging to a
church family that worshiped, grew, and served together never occurred
to him.

Another conversation took place with a young couple who was
married in the church. When the pastor asked about their plan for
church involvement, they agreed that church would be something they
added to their lives after they had children. The pastor failed to convince them that adding church to their schedules later would be difficult if they were not already in the habit of attending. They saw no
reason to attend before starting a family.

These three people saw church mostly as a consumable conven-
ience, memorable when they wanted something, forgettable when they
did not. They did not know church as a family, a community to which
they could contribute. The joy of serving with a community that shares

a common bond can be amazing. By giving more, these people could have lived fuller, richer lives.

What is even more amazing is how that bond reaches across congregational and denominational lines, so that all followers of Christ, of every creed, recognize one another as family members. I saw this reality in the fall of 2005, when the costliest and one of the strongest hurricanes in recorded history, Katrina, struck the Gulf Coast. Entire communities were completely devastated.

Our church quickly mobilized teams to respond. When our teams arrived, they soon noticed that they were not the first ones there. Several other vans and buses filled the street, and by the signs on the vehicles we saw that we were joining Nazarenes, Catholics, Baptists, and a myriad of others. Though the havoc of the destruction was disheartening, this scene of fellow laborers gave a glimpse of the Kingdom of God. Our church group prepared and fed lunch to the workers. Others brought tools and resources so that our work together was as effective and efficient as possible. All contributed skills as well as sweat, so that together we made a significant impact on that small region of the world. As we served, we forgot about doctrinal or style differences and remembered that we all serve the same God and live in the same needy world.

What is the Church? It's the body of Christ, doing what Christ would be doing if he were here physically on earth. People need the Church, because following Jesus was never meant to be a solo journey. We need one another. The Church celebrates with us, grieves with us, lifts us up, and helps us be the best versions of ourselves that we can possibly be. The Church is the way Jesus joins his followers together as a family.

- When have you seen the Church in action and been amazed at how God brings us all together?
- What is unique about your church? Of all the churches in your area, why should someone choose yours?

DAY SIX

MEMBERS ONLY

*He gave some apostles, some prophets, some evangelists, and
some pastors and teachers. His purpose was to equip God's
people for the work of serving and building up the body of
Christ until we all reach the unity of faith and knowledge of
God's Son. God's goal is for us to become mature adults—to
be fully grown, measured by the standard of the fullness of
Christ.*

Ephesians 4:11-13

Consider for a moment what it means to belong to your particular
church. When you joined the church, what kinds of questions did
your pastor ask? Membership expectations vary from denomination to
denomination, and from local church to local church. What we share in
common is an understanding of our call to be the body of Christ. If you
are a member of a community committed to care for one another and
encourage one another to grow in grace and knowledge, and that shares
the good news of Jesus Christ with a hurting world, then you have a role
to play in your particular setting.

If you became a member of a country club, health center, or even
a credit card program, you know that membership has many privileges.
When you join a church, however, you are more likely to lose privileges
than to gain them, because God asks us to give as well as to receive.
You lose the privilege to park closest to the building, even when it is
raining or snowing, and begin to park as far out as possible so the closest parking spaces are available for first-time visitors. You give up your
seat in the sanctuary if needed so that a visitor can sit down. You give
up the anonymity of being able to attend worship sporadically or as
your schedule permits. You take on greater responsibility for serving
both inside and outside the walls of the church. And, you make a commitment to share your financial resources to support the ministry and
mission of the church.

Belonging to a particular local church is a covenant relationship. We declare that we will support that church with our prayers, presence, gifts, and service. We commit to grow each day as we seek full transformation into Christlikeness—being fully alive in Christ.

Notice that today's Scripture speaks about how our gifts work in community. *The Message* paraphrase of this passage says that we move "rhythmically and easily with each other." This journey of faith is not something we do alone. We do it in the context of Christian community and in response to the calling of Christ.

What does it mean to you personally to belong to your particular church, in your community? Do you give yourself to the mission and work of your church, or do you stay on the perimeter, assuming you don't have much to contribute? The goal for our spiritual lives is to grow up and become mature Christians who live out the vision that God has for our work as the Church.

- What does it mean to you to belong to a church?
- How would you tell someone on the outside what it means to join your particular church?

.

WEEK 3
MAKING VISITORS FEEL
WELCOME

DAY ONE

INVENTIVE HOSPITALITY

Don't burn out; keep yourselves fueled and aflame. Be alert
servants of the Master, cheerfully expectant. Don't quit in hard
times; pray all the harder. Help needy Christians; be inventive
in hospitality.

Romans 12:11-13, *THE MESSAGE*

In Week One, we looked at what it means to be a relentlessly
outward-focused church. Week Two readings answered three major
questions regarding why we put effort toward evangelism in the first
place. This week we are going to look at how, as a church, we live out
the call to be welcoming and hospitable to anyone who walks through
our doors.

Remember the popular 1980s sitcom *Cheers*? The song communicates something about the human need to belong. We want to go
where everybody knows our name. We all love to walk through a door
and be recognized, a place where we can be ourselves. Consider that
most people will find some way to connect in this way, be it at a bar, a
church, an athletic club, or some other location.We are wired with a
need to belong. So how do we ensure that people who walk into our
church will feel a sense of belonging and being at home?

Today's Scripture reading spurs us to be "inventive" in our efforts
toward hospitality. Sometimes as churches we burn out and lose our
focus. We tend to hang out our OPEN sign and expect that people will
wander in and understand what to do next. But if we want to be thriv-
ing, growing, dynamic churches who are living out the mission to
which Jesus called us, we have to become a little more inventive than
that. We have to see every part of our church's ministries through the
eyes of a first-time visitor. We have to create an atmosphere where people walk in and feel at home. We have to stop doing some of the things
we currently do and start doing some new things in order to become
inventive in hospitality.

Make a few notes in the book margin about your church's current state of hospitality and welcome. Are you fueled and aflame, cheerfully expectant, and in prayer for those who may come to your church? Do you think a visitor who walks in will feel welcome and know what to do and where to go? Is there an overall sense of belonging among those gathered?

Compare your notes with your very best customer service experience. Maybe you frequent your favorite restaurant just for the service. Maybe you stay at a certain hotel when you travel because of the standard of hospitality. What aspects of those experiences can be applied to hospitality in the church? How can we take care of people who come in so that they are truly free to experience the love and grace of God through Jesus Christ?

As you go through this week, become a student of great customer service and hospitality. Keep notes about how you were made to feel valued, accepted, and welcome. Also, make notes about any bad experiences you have with hospitality this week and how it made you feel. Rememer that your church can be a community gathering place where people come to love and be loved, to know and be known. Begin to pray now, all the harder, for God to transform your congregation into an outward-focused, welcoming community.

- What ideas do you have for hospitality in your church that are "inventive"?
- How can your church avoid burnout in its ministry to welcome new members?

Day Two

Worship as a Second Language

After all, brothers and sisters, if I come to you speaking in tongues, how will I help you unless I speak to you with a revelation, some knowledge, a prophecy, or a teaching? Likewise, things that aren't alive like a harp or a lyre can make a sound, but if there aren't different notes in the sounds they make, how will the tune from the harp or the lyre be recognized? And if a trumpet call is unrecognizable, then who will prepare for battle? It's the same way with you: If you don't use language that is easy to understand when you speak in a tongue, then how will anyone understand what is said? It will be as if you are speaking into the air! There are probably many language families in the world, and none of them are without meaning. So if I don't know the meaning of the language, then I will be like a foreigner to those who speak it, and they will be like foreigners to me. The same holds true for you: since you are ambitious for spiritual gifts, use your ambition to try to work toward being the best at building up the church.

1 Corinthians 14:6-12

Imagine dressing up for a night at the symphony. You get there early to stroll around the terrace. When the chimes sound, you quickly go to your seat. The orchestra members take their places, followed by the concertmaster, who begins the tuning. The audience erupts in applause as the conductor enters and calls the orchestra to attention. With the first beat of the baton, the musicians begin to play—whatever each of them feels like playing at that moment. Some people in the audience look on as though they are hearing beautiful music. Others cover their ears, because to them the sound is simply noise.

In today's Bible reading, Paul explains the importance of both hearing and understanding. For first-time visitors in church, worship can be like that symphony concert. People around them are participating and following along in step. But the visitors may be apprehensive about what happens next and may ultimately disengage from the experience. Worship should be the place where visitors feel, most, like they belong; but for many it is the place where they feel most excluded. When I travel and attend worship, I often find myself confused as to when to sit, pray, sing, or listen. This is in part because I don't understand the "language" of those churches. Our worship gatherings can seem like a foreign language to those who were not raised in the church. But there are ways to welcome those visitors as honored guests and make them feel at home.

In order to make visitors feel welcome in our worship gatherings, we don't have to do away with our traditions and history. We don't have to water down our beliefs to meet the needs of newcomers. What we have to do is imagine being a new person in our midst, for whom our worship service is not their first language.

How might we engage and explain, to help visitors follow along and understand? Maybe your pastors introduce themselves every week or explain why we pray together the Lord's Prayer. Maybe they make a special point to welcome visitors and invite them to come just as they are and to feel at home. Maybe the church forms a team of people who do all they can to make sure visitors know what to do and where to go to find what they need.

All church members should help to make visitors feel at home and welcome. The goal is for visitors to hear the music and message, not just noise.

- How well do you think a first-time visitor would understand your worship gathering?
- What can you do to be the best at building up the church?

DAY THREE

MARYS AND MARTHAS

While Jesus and his disciples were traveling, Jesus entered a village where a woman named Martha welcomed him as a guest. She had a sister named Mary, who sat at the Lord's feet and listened to his message. By contrast, Martha was preoccupied with getting everything ready for their meal. So Martha came to him and said, "Lord, don't you care that my sister has left me to prepare the table all by myself? Tell her to help me."

The Lord answered, "Martha, Martha, you are worried and distracted by many things. One thing is necessary. Mary has chosen the better part. It won't be taken away from her."

Luke 10:38-41

For almost everyone who reads this Bible passage, we relate either to Mary, the one who noticed the sense of the moment and sat at Jesus' feet to learn, commune, and soak it in; or to Martha, the one who ran about the house making sure things were picked up and that there was food to eat and oil in the lamps. You might even be a Mary in some situations and a Martha in others. Whichever character you relate to most, this passage has so much to teach us about hospitality and welcome.

First, let's look at Mary. The Scripture says that she "sat at the Lord's feet and listened to his message." She must have felt the weight of what it meant, to have Jesus sitting in her living room, teaching and spending time with her. She knew it was a rare moment, and she wanted to be fully present. Maybe she realized she had a long list of chores. She probably knew that Martha was getting irritated. She even may have wondered if she should get up and help. But to Mary, just being with Jesus far outweighed any other thing.

Now, let's see it from Martha's perspective. Someone had to clean the house. Someone had to make sure there would be light in the evening. Someone had to prepare food. Someone had to see that the guests felt at home and got what they needed. If Martha had sat down at Jesus' feet, then who would have provided the hospitality?

This was probably an unexpected gathering for which Martha and Mary were unprepared. Yes, Martha could have sat at Jesus' feet and expected that Jesus would make sure, in his miraculous ways, that there would be light and food and comfort. And Mary could have helped a little and listened to Jesus at the same time. But hear what Jesus says is the root of the issue: Martha was distracted by the surprise gathering and by all the practical things that needed to be done.

What about our churches? They are filled with Mary types and Martha types. How can we work together to be prepared when we have an opportunity to show hospitality? Marys can help us be present in the moment, to see opportunities for real connection. They can help us work ahead, to get things in order so that when the time arrives we are free to host the gathering without distraction. Marthas can help us tend to the details, to see the work that needs to be done and help us get to it.

We are distracted by many things. It is important work to make sure that our church is always ready and inviting. You just never know who might show up.

- Are you a Mary, a Martha, or a combination of the two?
- What tasks can your church handle ahead of time to make a hospitable and welcoming environment for anyone who walks through your doors?

DAY FOUR

CARING FOR THE DETAILS

Open your homes to each other without complaining.
1 Peter 4:9

Each year my family spends a week during the winter in Florida. For a Midwesterner, time in the Florida sun during the winter is a treasured experience. One of the favorite activities for my husband and son is to head out with some extended family members and fish in one of the local jetties. They love getting up early in the morning, packing lunches and snacks, making a day of it, and we look forward to enjoying their prize of grouper, red fish, and trigger fish. This past winter, they decided to try catching grouper by using shrimp as bait.

They settled on the jetty and baited their hooks with the shrimp. Within seconds my brother-in-law's pole dipped deep into the water, signaling the bite of a fish, and then his second pole dipped. You can imagine how excited he was. He spent the next few hours attracting and reeling in fish after fish. My stepfather, on the other hand, was not getting a bite. What was going on? They were fishing in the same location, with the same bait. Finally, in exasperation, my stepfather asked my brother-in-law what he was doing to attract so many fish, and he discovered the trick. My brother-in-law had taken an extra step preparing his bait. My stepfather had been putting the shrimp from his bait bucket right on the hook, while my brother-in-law had taken the time to peel each shrimp carefully, making it more inviting to the fish. This extra step increased his effectiveness.

Attention to detail is how we offer that next level of hospitality in our churches. When we do the little extra things, newcomers have an experience that makes them want to return. According to research, visitors decide in three to eight minutes whether or not they'll return to a church. First impressions matter to people who may be nervous about coming to church for the first time or to people who are looking for a new place to worship and grow. A first-time visitor begins forming impressions about your congregation even before getting out of the car. These impressions are made by the appearance of your facilities and grounds, the quality of your signage, the congestion in your parking lot, the friendliness of your congregation, and the cleanliness of your nursery, to name only a few factors.

Recently we had the church trustees tour our facilities with the eyes of a first-time visitor. They had digital cameras and were asked to take pictures of anything they saw that would be unattractive or confusing to a first-time visitor. They discovered poor directional signage, peeling paint, stained carpet and ceiling tiles, potholes in the parking lot, unsightly landscaping, and disorganized and dingy nurseries that were difficult to access.

So what are the details that need attention at your church? How might God be leading you to fix up the place so that newcomers experience an "at-home" feeling from the minute they enter the parking lot?

Now, to be sure, fixing up little things is not a glamorous ministry. Pulling weeds, filling cracks, cleaning toys, and posting signs don't necessarily feel like God's work. However, these are the details that help visitors feel at home. When we invite outsiders in, we are opening our church home to them. Let us not grumble about the work, but instead joyfully make preparations for our guests.

- What needs to be done around your church?
- What gifts do you have for attention to details?

Day Five

Change for the Better

*The Lord is the Spirit, and where the Lord's Spirit is, there is
freedom. All of us are looking with unveiled faces at the glory
of the Lord as if we were looking in a mirror. We are being
transformed into that same image from one degree of glory to
the next degree of glory. This comes from the Lord, who is the
Spirit.*

2 Corinthians 3:17-18

Remember Ebenezer Scrooge? Long before Dr. Seuss brought the
Grinch into being, Charles Dickens created Scrooge, who played
a prominent role in A Christmas Carol. Scrooge taught the English-
speaking world to proclaim, "Bah! Humbug!" He was, wrote Dickens,
"a squeezing, wrenching, grasping, scraping, clutching, covetous old
sinner! Hard and sharp as flint, from which no steel had ever struck out
generous fire; secret, and self contained, and solitary as an oyster. The
cold within him froze his old features . . . and spoke out shrewdly in his
grating voice."

But Scrooge changed. Oh, how he changed! By the end of the
story, he was giving away coins, buying the biggest turkey in the
butcher's window for poor Bob Cratchit and his family, promising to
care for Tiny Tim, and smiling at everyone he met. "He became as good
a friend, as good a master, and as good a man, as the good old city
knew, or any other good old city, town or borough, in the good old
world." And all it took was one long, long night spent with the ghosts
of Christmas Past, Christmas Present, and Christmas Future.

Your journey into the deep waters of faith is even bigger and better
than old Scrooge's. As we change from who we are now to the person
God would have us to be, we are promised the Holy Spirit as our guide
and companion. As we take on the image of Jesus Christ, we begin to
see with his eyes. We see our churches for the ministries they are called
to live out. We see people who don't attend church as lost sheep who

need rescue. We see our faith growing in ways we couldn't have imagined. We know we are growing because of our eagerness to serve. Our spiritual growth comes from our search for true transformation, the kind that only Jesus can give us.

In Philippians 2:12-13, we are called to "make every effort" as we do God's work in our churches, our communities, and our world. A change in us is only evidenced by a change in our behavior, our willingness to give and serve, and our attitude. While some living creatures can literally grow out of their skin and take on a new one, we don't always have a tangible sense of growth. But, like Ebenezer Scrooge, our growth can be demonstrated by how we live. Scrooge became a generous, loving man. When we come to know the love of Jesus and choose to follow him, we begin to transform into his likeness. As that happens, we begin to see with his eyes and look for opportunities to share his love with everyone we meet.

- In what ways are you growing in faith and discipleship?
- How is your spiritual growth evidenced by the way you live?

Day Six

What Will You Do?

*He gave some apostles, some prophets, some evangelists, and
some pastors and teachers. His purpose was to equip God's
people for the work of serving and building up the body of
Christ until we all reach the unity of faith and knowledge of
God's Son. God's goal is for us to become mature adults—to
be fully grown, measured by the standard of the fullness of
Christ. As a result, we aren't supposed to be infants any longer
who can be tossed and blown around by every wind that comes
from teaching with deceitful scheming and the tricks people
play to deliberately mislead others. Instead, by speaking the
truth with love, let's grow in every way into Christ, who is the
head. The whole body grows from him, as it is joined and held
together by all the supporting ligaments. The body makes itself
grow in that it builds itself up with love as each one does their
part.*

Ephesians 4:11-16

Personal trainers, sports coaches, and physical education teachers
will tell you that to be truly fit and healthy, you must take care of
the entire body. A strong core benefits running, strong legs help support
the back, and any kind of endurance training trims fat from the body.
We hear over and over that "spot training"—training only a few mus-
cles and ignoring the rest—is not effective for any athlete.

The same is true for the body of Christ. Each and every part of the
Body is essential, and when one part suffers, or is ignored, the whole
Body is less than it could be. You are a part of this Body, and need to
care for your own spiritual life. Like your physical diet, your spiritual
diet will help to nourish you. It should include worship, daily Scripture
reading, and participating in a small group. We also are fed by the
presence of the community through our prayers and our care for one
another.

Just as knowledge is important in caring for our physical bodies, learning about your role in the Body is also essential. Understanding what this role is, though, may not be immediately apparent. Maybe you see yourself more as an observer, as someone who comes and is fed by the community but does not play a vital role in the ministry. The truth, though, is that God has gifted you with skills and talents that can play an important role in building up others in the church, spreading the good news of God's love, and bringing healing to the world.

A healthy body requires regular exercise. A good diet and knowledge of how to care for the body are useless if they are never used. In the same way, preparing our minds for ministry and understanding our gifts and skills mean nothing if we do not put them to good use.

Our Scripture passage today tells us that Christ equipped people so they can equip others in the community to become mature in faith, move toward unity, and help others grow, building them up in love. Being a member of a Christian community is important. It helps us grow individually and as a group. But there are also responsibilities that come with being a member of the body of Christ.

What part of the Body are you? What role is yours in the body of Christ? You may already know how God has gifted you. You may be using your gifts in your work, your home, another organization, or even the church. You may also have some undiscovered natural abilities. You now have the opportunity to learn how you might use these gifts as a member of the body of Christ in your church.

The best way is simply to get involved. Do not wait to be asked. Instead, look for a place where you think you could help. If you wait or procrastinate, you are missing opportunities. And the church is missing out on what you have to offer.

When you become an active part of the body of Christ, you help the church to become, fully, what Christ intends, and when the church is unified and building people up in love, others will want to be a part of it. In the end, this is what we are to be about as a church. We are to be a witness and a light reaching out to the world.

- How are you exercising your gifts in the church?
- What does it mean to build up the church in love?

WEEK 4
INVITING OTHERS TO GROW IN FAITH

DAY ONE

NOT TO BE SERVED, BUT TO SERVE

*Jesus called them over and said, "You know that the ones who
are considered the rulers by the Gentiles show off their au-
thority over them and their high-ranking officials order them
around. But that's not the way it will be with you. Whoever
wants to be great among you will be your servant. Whoever
wants to be first among you will be the slave of all, for the
Human One didn't come to be served but rather to serve and
to give his life to liberate many people."*

Mark 10:42-45

Imagine that the biggest celebrity you can think of has announced
that he or she is going to visit your town, and you are in charge of all
the arrangements. And this will not be an in-and-out, ninety-minute
visit; it will be a stay of several weeks, perhaps months. You're probably thinking about the best restaurants, the most comfortable lodging,
a schedule that includes meetings with leading citizens, and luxurious
transportation, because you are quite sure that is what your guest will
expect. If someone said, "I'll lend you my pup tent and camp stove,
and we can set things up in the vacant lot next to the laundromat," you
would no doubt turn down that offer without a second thought.

Consider how things went when God, the creator and ruler of the
universe, came to earth as a human being, a Galilean named Jesus. You
may be familiar with the story. Jesus was born in a stable and slept in
an animal-feeding trough filled with straw. He grew up in a backwater
town called Nazareth, a place with a bad reputation. Though he was a
compelling speaker who drew large crowds, he never showed any interest in profiting financially. In fact, he once said of himself, "Foxes
have holes and birds have nests, but the Son of Man has no place to
lay his head" (Luke 9:58). He chose uneducated working people as his
closest associates, rather than reaching out to those who could have
opened doors for him through their connections. One of his followers

betrayed him, and the authorities who led the Roman occupation force in Palestine executed him. When he died, he had nothing of his own and was buried in a borrowed tomb. Christians are convinced he rose from this tomb on the third day, and the rest is history.

Jesus said he did not come to be served, but to serve. The story of his life bears that out. He used his powers in quiet acts of blessing and restoration. He directed his teaching to anyone who would listen. He showed a special affinity for the poor and powerless, those who needed him far more than he needed them. An early Christian hymn quoted by the apostle Paul in his letter to the Philippians honored this reality, asking followers of Jesus to "adopt the attitude that was in Christ Jesus":

> Though he was in the form of God,
> he did not consider being equal with God something to exploit.
> But he emptied himself
> by taking the form of a slave
> and by becoming like human beings.
> When he found himself in the form of a human,
> he humbled himself by becoming obedient to the point of
> death, even death on a cross.
> Therefore, God highly honored him
> and gave him a name above all names,
> so that at the name of Jesus everyone
> in heaven, on earth, and under the earth might bow
> and every tongue confess that
> Jesus Christ is Lord, to the glory of God the Father.
>
> Philippians 2: 6-11

Did you catch how Paul introduced that hymn? "Adopt the attitude that was in Christ Jesus." When we follow Jesus, we are called to be servants, just as he was. Christianity has never been a "what's in it for me" kind of faith. Not all of Jesus' followers through the centuries have lived in poverty; not all have been obscure and unknown. But all of Jesus' true followers share this central characteristic: they have a servant's heart. Their primary question and focus is "How can I serve and bless others?" rather than "How can I get others to serve and bless me?"

God equips each of us to serve in various ways. Whatever our station in life, whatever position we hold, we are called to the highest position and the greatest honor God can bestow; we are called to be servants.

- In what ways has God called you to serve?
- What unique gifts do you bring to the community?

Day Two

We Are the Body

A demonstration of the Spirit is given to each person for the common good. . . . Christ is just like the human body—a body is a unit and has many parts; and all the parts of the body are one body, even though there are many. We were all baptized by one Spirit into one body, whether Jew or Greek, or slave or free, and we all were given one Spirit to drink. Certainly the body isn't one part but many. If the foot says, "I'm not part of the body because I'm not a hand," does that mean it's not part of the body? If the ear says, "I'm not part of the body because I'm not an eye," does that mean it's not part of the body? If the whole body were an eye, what would happen to the hearing? And if the whole body were an ear, what would happen to the sense of smell? But as it is, God has placed each one of the parts in the body just like he wanted.

1 Corinthians 12:7, 12-18

When we talk about God calling each one of us to be a servant, many people feel a discouraging sense of being overwhelmed. Their inner thoughts may sound similar to this:

I know! I should serve at a soup kitchen every week. I should teach children how to read, or tell them Bible stories. I should visit a nursing home. I should go to Africa. I should give more to charity, lead the United Way campaign at work, donate my extra clothes to Goodwill, and sign up to work with children who have special needs. I should take a meal to the homeless guy I see on the street corner every day. I should volunteer in the nursery at church. I should sign up to serve as an usher or sing in the choir. But I don't have the time and energy to do all those things. And I don't even want to do a lot of them. God, forgive me.

Others who are less conscientious may think, "Service? I am way too busy for that."

The Bible has a message for both kinds of people, and all of us who fall somewhere in between. We can summarize the message like this: God has equipped every one of us to serve; therefore no one can say, "I have no gifts." But God has made us each to serve in specific ways, not to do everything in general. Because each of us is unique, you can serve in certain ways and places that no one else can fill quite like you. Nothing else you do in life will bring you the joy and satisfaction that comes from finding that special, personal kind of service that fits you.

We are the body of Christ, made up of many parts, and even parts that seem similar make their own unique contribution. For example, most of us have two eyes. You may think of your eyes as identical, but in fact each one makes a unique contribution to your eyesight, as you will discover if you ever try to play Ping-Pong with one eye covered. Depth perception depends on each eye providing its unique perspective.

In a similar way, each of us is equipped to function not as the whole body of Christ, but as one member of the Body, with a distinct contribution to make. An ear may not be capable of swinging a hammer but will have a wonderful capacity for listening. The fine points of art are rendered easily with a hand but may completely escape a foot, whose ability to carry burdens and provide balance are essential to the entire body.

Paul adds that these gifts are for the common good. In the young church at Corinth to whom this letter was addressed, it appears the members had begun to fight with one another. Some were discounting the importance of others' gifts while magnifying their own. This is why Paul imagines the absurd situation of a foot envying the hands and trying to "secede" from the body because it does not get to do what they do. Clearly, the church had lost its focus. They were looking inward at themselves instead of looking outward, together.

Until we understand our unique contribution to the common good, we may get caught up envying the gifts of others. Sure, the face gets noticed before the forearm, but every gift adds to the good and keeps the church focused and working effectively toward its mission to reach the world with the good news of Jesus Christ.

- How have you envied the gifts of others?
- What part do you play in the common good?

Day Three

Discover Your Gifts to Serve

Brothers and sisters, I don't want you to be ignorant about spiritual gifts.... There are different spiritual gifts but the same Spirit; and there are different ministries and the same Lord; and there are different activities but the same God who produces all of them in everyone.

1 Corinthians 12:1, 4-6

Remember how exciting Christmas was when you were a kid? There were so many mysterious packages, or maybe that one big one with a funny shape you could not figure out. Most families have a special time to open packages and finally see what is inside.

Maybe you are feeling at least a little bit of that same anticipation as we approach today's subject—I hope so. It is a powerful, exciting thing to understand more clearly how you are made, what things contribute to your uniqueness, and where God has equipped you to serve. For some people, this discovery is literally life-changing.

Discovering your gifts is a three-step process:

1. Explore

First, learn what the Bible teaches about your uniqueness, and how your spiritual gifts shape that uniqueness for service to God and others. This book offers a few quick glimpses, but dig deeper. Look for a study on spiritual gifts that will help you identify the gifts God placed in you. *Serving from the Heart*, by Carol Cartmill and Yvonne Gentile, is a great place to start.

2. Experience

Once you have discovered your gifts, look for ways to use them. If you wonder what you might be good at or be gifted to do, you can always try out different ministries in your church. Maybe you would love to be a greeter and welcome people who enter your church doors. Maybe you would love to deliver small gifts to first-time visitors and let them know how glad you are that they came to visit. As the *Catch* teams in your church begin to carry out the practices of invitational evangelism, there will be many opportunities and places for you to explore your gifts.

You cannot discover with certainty that you have a spiritual gift simply by reading a book or taking a class. Get your hands dirty! Look for ways to use your gifts to bless others and to honor God. As you get involved in action, watch for two things in particular that will help you determine whether you are actually putting your gifts to work. First, watch for effectiveness. If you are using one of your gifts, the gift should "work." If you are trying to teach, people should be learning. If you are trying to show mercy, people should feel comforted and blessed. This does not mean you will immediately be an expert in your gift, but it does mean that you should see effectiveness. Second, watch for an inner sense of joy and rightness. Using your gifts will often stretch you, taking you far beyond your comfort zone. Service will not always be easy, and you will not always be happy while doing it. But if you are moving in the right direction, you will experience a deep sense that "this is what I was made for." And the joy that comes from that feeling is profound.

3. Be Encouraged

If you are using your gifts, watch for and expect that other members of the body of Christ will encourage and affirm you. Be alert to this, because it is one of the ways the church works together. Each of us has a part to play, but all of us build one another up.

- How is God revealing gifts in you?
- How might your gifts build up the church?

DAY FOUR

YOUR GIFTEDNESS AND GOD'S WILL

So, brothers and sisters, because of God's mercies, I encourage you to present your bodies as a living sacrifice that is holy and pleasing to God. This is your appropriate priestly service. Don't be conformed to the patterns of this world, but be transformed by the renewing of your minds so that you can figure out what God's will is—what is good and pleasing and mature.

Because of the grace that God gave me, I can say to each one of you: don't think of yourself more highly than you ought to think. Instead be reasonable since God has measured out a portion of faith to each one of you. We have many parts in one body, but the parts don't all have the same function. In the same way, though there are many of us, we are one body in Christ, and individually we belong to each other. We have different gifts that are consistent with God's grace that has been given to us. If your gift is prophecy, you should prophesy in proportion to your faith. If your gift is service, devote yourself to serving. If your gift is teaching, devote yourself to teaching. If your gift is encouragement, devote yourself to encouraging. The one giving should do it with no strings attached. The leader should lead with passion. The one showing mercy should be cheerful.

Romans 12:1-8

There are typically two types of classes in school. There are the core courses, which are the things all students are expected to learn, and then there are the electives. Core courses are required, and students cannot graduate without taking them. Electives, such as badminton, basket-weaving, or barn architecture in the American Midwest, are offered for students who want to take them; but obviously students can fulfill all the requirements for graduation without having badminton on their transcript.

Many Christians consider learning about their giftedness for service as a church elective. They may believe this subject to be interesting or fun but do not believe it matters whether they take the class. In today's Bible passage, we see that the apostle Paul considered it important. He viewed understanding giftedness as a core course, with the clear-cut reason that understanding your giftedness is a key way to understand God's will for your life.

Paul begins with a stirring call to serve God: "Present your bodies as a living sacrifice that is holy and pleasing to God." Paul describes this as true worship, which communicates clearly that worship is not just something we do once a week in a church building. He calls us to be transformed and says that by surrendering to God in this way, we "can figure out what God's will is—what is good and pleasing and mature." I want to know God's will. Don't you?

But that is a lofty goal. How do I offer myself as a living sacrifice, doing God's will each day? As though to answer that question directly, Paul writes, "Don't think of yourself more highly than you ought to think. Instead be reasonable since God has measured out a portion of faith to each one of you." To understand and live God's will for us, he continues, we need to think of ourselves accurately. We should not think too highly of ourselves, as though the whole weight of the world rested on us. Neither should we think of ourselves as people with nothing to offer. Instead, we need to "be reasonable" about our place and our contribution.

Suppose a friend who has recently moved into a newly built home is planning to host an open house and asks you for help, stating, "The driveway needs to be swept, the windows need washing, and some loose boards need to be nailed down." You agree to help. When you arrive, your friend is swamped. Because you know each other well, he does not initiate conversation but rather simply hands you a broom and says, "Thanks." You're not going to stand there wondering what to do, wishing your friend could have verbally communicated his wishes, are you? And you're not going to waste time and energy trying to wash the windows with a broom! You're going to go sweep the driveway, prompted by the equipment that your friend handed you.

Romans 12 says one of the best ways to know God's will for your life is to look at the equipment God has handed you. Think reasonably about yourself and your gifts, and you will have a good idea of where and how God wants you to serve. Then, deploy those gifts. Don't wait for the church to tell you what to do. Look for opportunities to match up your passions and skills, and start serving.

- What tools has God handed you to serve with?
- What opportunities are there in your church to use your gifts in service?

Day Five

It Might Not Be What You Think

Because they missed this goal, some people have been distracted by talk that doesn't mean anything. They want to be teachers of Law without understanding either what they are saying or what they are talking about with such confidence.

1 Timothy 1:6-7

A friend tells about a man who worked all of his life as a doctor. For much of the time this man hated his job. He looked forward to days off and could hardly wait for vacations. He retired as soon as he was able, and he promised himself he would never make hospital calls again if he could help it. Retirement, however, did not bring him automatic happiness. He still had a lot of anger as well as some destructive habits. With some encouragement from his wife, he decided to get involved with a church, something he had decided against years earlier. After some searching, they joined a church.

Transformation did not happen all at once, but this man began to change. He found the power to set aside his destructive habits. He found an outlet for his love of music by joining the choir. He learned that God was calling him to service, and he began to explore what gifts he might have. He talked with one of the pastors about how he could help with the work of offering spiritual care and support to others in the church. The pastor told him she thought he would be good at visiting members in the hospital, and encouraging and praying with them. His immediate response was, "No! I want to help, but not in that way." But the pastor did not back off. Her suggestion was not random; she honestly felt that she was discerning a special giftedness in him for that kind of service.

Finally, with reluctance, he agreed to try. He was startled to find he did not hate this particular form of service, but instead found it a blessing. Additionally, he almost instantly received affirmation from the church members he visited. Now he makes hospital calls several times a week, and he loves it. He has a deep sense of calling about his ministry. He knows that he is using his giftedness to serve others and bring glory to God. A smile lights his face when he talks about making hospital calls. He has found the unique place of service that God equipped him to fill.

I know people who have always loved the comforts of home yet now eagerly look forward to the chance to spend time in Honduras or South Africa, blessing those who live in uncomfortable conditions. I know people who used to say, "I never read a book," who now eagerly look forward to leading Bible studies and going deep into the questions that arise in their classes. I know people who used to live to make money who now find great joy in giving away large amounts of their money to bless others.

A distinguished religious teacher named Nicodemus came to see Jesus. He expected to ask some textbook questions, get some textbook answers, and go home to resume his life. Instead, he found himself immediately challenged, stretched, and confused by Jesus' words. Sensing his consternation, Jesus said, "Don't be so surprised when I tell you that you have to be 'born from above'—out of this world, so to speak. You know well enough how the wind blows this way and that. You hear it rustling through the trees, but you have no idea where it comes from or where it's headed next. That's the way it is with everyone 'born from above' by the wind of God, the Spirit of God" (John 3:7-8, *THE MESSAGE*).

Set out to find your gifts and your unique ministry—the one no one can live out quite like you can. Be open to God's Spirit, and let the wind blow you in the direction God wants you to go.

- Share stories of people you know who discovered their gifts and now joyfully serve.
- Ponder your own gifts—those you know about and those you hope to discover—and imagine how you might use them to do God's work.

DAY SIX

CATCH A NEW LIFE

And now, little children, remain in relationship to Jesus, so that
when he appears we can have confidence and not be ashamed
in front of him when he comes.

1 John 2:28

The score of the semifinal game in the Kansas State 6A high school playoffs was 17 to 14. The trailing Falcons had the ball on their opponent's 26 yard line as the clock ticked away the final minutes of the game. It was fourth and ten. If the Falcons failed to move the ball ten yards, the season would be over. The play was called: "62-God!" The crowd stood on its feet in anticipation. The quarterback looked right then left, and he released the ball. As the ball sailed into the air, all eyes in both stands followed to see where it would go. Then the unexpected happened—the ball had been thrown to the wide receiver, who was running toward the end zone fighting off double coverage. The receiver looked back over his left shoulder, lunged forward fully extending his body, and with outstretched arms caught the ball for the game-winning touchdown.

The newspaper editorial in the sports section the next day called it the "catch of the year," and to this day we still refer to it as the "catch of a lifetime." The wide receiver was my son, and I know firsthand the complete exhilaration and joy he felt making that catch. It is indeed something he will remember for a lifetime.

There are several notable factors to consider in this story:

1. The quarterback and receiver were part of a team in which each member had an important job to do in order to make that play possible.
2. The quarterback threw the ball expecting it to be caught. He had confidence in his wide receiver. They had developed a plan for this play, and now was the time to make it happen.

3. The wide receiver was in position, ready to receive the ball with outstretched hands.

For the past four weeks you have been diving into deep waters, thinking about what it means to fish for people, to be a relentlessly outward-focused church with a passion for reaching lost people. You have discovered that you have an important job in the work of the church when it comes to reaching and connecting people. Throughout this journey, you have been led to ask yourself, "What does it mean for me?" Now is the time to seek God's direction and make it happen. If catching a football can bring joy, imagine the joy God has in store for you as you find your special place in the work of reaching people for Jesus Christ. All God requires is that you be in position and ready to receive, with outstretched hands and open arms. Discovering your place in the work of the kingdom is the true catch of a lifetime.

- What does it mean to have outstretched arms when God calls you?
- What has challenged you the most about discerning your place in becoming an outward focused congregation?

MINISTRY DESCRIPTIONS
AND COMMITMENT FORM

After participating in the *Catch* program, I am compelled to join a ministry team and get to work fishing for people. I understand that Jesus calls us to seek the least and the lost, and that means becoming an outward-focused church. I would like to join the following team:

_____Connection Point Ministry
Learning about church ministries and programs in order to connect visitors and members to them. Staffing the Connection Point desk and directing persons to their desired locations.

_____Mugging Ministry
Regularly delivering mugs / gifts as well as information about the church to first-time visitors. Volunteers will specify their delivery area and pick up mugs from a designated location each week.

_____Traffic Ministry
Perhaps working in conjunction with the trustees or building committee, this group will ensure adequate parking and assistance in the parking lot. In addition, this team will ensure that signage is clear and helpful from the minute a visitor pulls into the parking lot.

_____Marketing / Communications Ministry
This team will ensure that clear, thoughtful, well-designed communication pieces are sent out.

_____Welcoming Worship Ministry
Perhaps in conjunction with the greeters, ushers, and pastoral staff, this team will ensure that persons are greeted at the door, assisted to a seat, and given helpful information. In addition, this team will help make every person in the worship space feel welcomed and invited to participate.

_____Phone Ministry
This team will make cold calls using provided lists, inviting persons to worship as well as to various programs and events throughout the year.

_____Coffee with the Pastors Ministry
This team will work with the pastors to create a welcoming experience in which visitors are encouraged to become members. This may include providing refreshments, setting up or tearing down, and occasionally giving a testimony about being a member of your church.

Name _____

Address _____

Phone _____

Email _____